MINK COAT

MINK COAT

poems by

Jill Hoffman

Holt, Rinehart and Winston

NEW YORK   CHICAGO   SAN FRANCISCO

Published simultaneously in Canada
by Holt, Rinehart and Winston of Canada, Limited.

ISBN (hardbound): 0-03-010956-6
ISBN (paperback): 0-03-010951-5
Library of Congress Catalog Card Number: 73-4200

First Edition

Designer: Andrew Roberts

Printed in the United States of America

Some of these poems originally appeared in the following
magazines whose editors are thanked for permission
to reprint: *American Review 16, Antaeus, Antioch Review,
Chelsea, Chicago Review, Contributor Magazine, Epoch,
Kenyon Review, New Republic, New York Quarterly,
Quarterly Review of Literature, Some, Transatlantic Review.*
"Horns" first appeared in *Unmuzzled Ox*, Volume I, No. 1,
copyright © 1971 by *Unmuzzled Ox*. Reprinted with their
permission. "Riverside Park" first appeared in *The New
Yorker* and is reprinted with their permission.

For my Mother and Father

Contents

(vii

A Fiery Furnace

I

(x

MINK COAT

Reader:

invisible to you
to whom I hint I am
a bellydancer,
in my spare time
sleeping with everyone,
I wear a body-
stocking
and come to your canopied
palanquin
in nothing but sequins
sewn to my bare skin,
a bright lampshade,
a tent for us
to loll in, a summer
night full of fireflies
singeing the hairshirt
you wear
to resist me,
until my veiled flesh
runs
its ladders up your
eyes
which open
on the page of this
world striped with welts
like a back
and you see me at last

Ice

Ice drips from the eaves of winter in beads
come loose from a crystal necklace spilling,
so that a girl would have to search April
and May on hands and knees to gather them
and never fill her empty handkerchief.
Let her fold all her days into a drawer
and all her nights into a lined basket
smoothing the neat piles with her careful strokes,
so that they will not slip away between
dreams, leaving her old and empty-handed.

O Hieronymus Bosch

O Hieronymus Bosch,
I think I am one of your creatures!
Last night before I went to sleep
his penis was my beak, slim buttocks
were my breasts, my long arms his legs.
And down below, as if sliced
by a strange reflecting pool,
my buttocks fleshed his leanness out with breasts
and my legs held him headless in a long kiss.

West Side

a fog fresh from London spills up the stairs
of the Chinese laundry on our block
—as if all your shirts, and my tablecloth, were burning!—
journeying
over the roofs of cars and the low hedges of
snow, into the glamorous spaces between
men with Russian mustaches that brush past me
steaming in the starchy night, stomping
casually uphill into the dilated meadows
of my eyes, dangerous as the curbs
where dogs squat brooding behind some back,
black spots in someone else's lung, something
stuck in the incinerator trying to get clear
                              —upstairs, the clouds
stare in a lighted mirror, saucy as salesgirls
modeling glass thimbles made of stars to cup the breasts,
someone is tracking me home with him like mud.

Dream

Safe and dreaming in your arms, sleep sends
a slow truck for me filled with odds and ends
on fire. I am jammed in with bodies and keep
the window shut so smoke will not escape
and leave me wide awake to burn. We creep
numbly to an oven we are already in,
grinding skulls, limbs, torsos, wedged and pinned.
Through the dim glass and rattling tin
your kisses enter, reprieving the condemned,
and cart me home to our own lovely bed,
where, drowsy, dumb, oblivious, the bright moon strews
smarting in our eyes the ashes of brilliant Jews.

Pietà

Forever cloistered in the crumpled car
with you unearthly in my arms
without your glasses, peaceful, painted
like an actor, for death,
my crushed leg aching under your fragile bulk,
your white shirt passionately red
with my blood, your child
in my womb hanging like a green fruit,
I cried out "Christ" and "Mama" to the holy ghost.

Mother,

while you fast in the country
on the third floor where no one
can reach you, I have broken
my diet in the city
and can't write a letter
because of being sick and sorry
for myself with the flu,
but wouldn't mention food anyway
to you, who are there to fool
all the doctors, change all
the cells in your body, to save
your breast—who can order you
home to sanity, to this . . .
only I walk around full of new
life that bunches and twists
like a pillow from the Oliver
Cromwell Hotel and I see the dead
eating pizza and returning with a
second shaking orange drink in
overcoats that have forgotten
the feel of flesh, and I think that
maybe when you give up food the angel
of death walks away in disgust,
admiration, despair, to eat
his own evanescent turds in the
garden of filth humans leave.

March Landscape

All the muted colors rinsed and clear
the cold day moons in birchlight, thuds
with rain on our old roof that will last
at least this spring—then we'll be gone.
Sad day, for all my coveting to capture
there is no snare, or song, to catch you in.
A repetition of some day last year,
your minute by minute ageless absorbing face
mocks the diminution that marks our lives.
Even last year's birds begin to fade
as they flit in gay flirtatious pairs
unentangled in the dripping net the trees
throw up against the sky, to fetch in a big haul.

Apartment

Here I must not use my powerful binoculars to see.
People nest in the windows, naked to the waist,
and on the crawling sidewalks down below, peck
at the black, suspect seeds the belching chimneys throw.
Children scribble the street like the colored chalk
they use to gild hours that the block is closed
and end erased, guttered away by rain or time.
The door of the small church on the corner
and the same-day cleaner's neon heart are red.
Misery from a distance resembles beauty.
The people I meet are trapped in marriages,
bruising the fruit they cannot give away.
Large families of their quarrels infest the walls
of this old building, whose coats and coats of paint
speak in a thickened tongue of better days.
I have cut off the hair that used to catch in branches
in the woods cobwebbed over in the bare month
since I left. A white bird crumples its wings
like newspaper the wind reads, like no bird
that ever chased in season through fresh air.
There is some demon who lures one to lean out
(far enough, and you can see the river!), despite reports
of suicides—meat dropping from heaven in a terrible
plenty—or children who perhaps thought they could fly.
Out there, even the babies in carriages are pushed by life.

Death II

Death lives on the East Side
in a penthouse
overlooking Central Park
with a view that draws him
out, and then back into
himself, skyline, reservoir
reminding him of
dreams to tell the doctor,
and the slew
of beautiful women he gets
is each fit to spend
a last night with.

In Time of Plague

I. RECEPTIONIST

There's an epidemic, she
said, her voice cutting
strings, unsealing
cartons,
and frankly if it was
Shakespeare . . .
she had had rabbis kneel
praying at her desk,
the last altar of the
despoiled,
her life threatened
by phone
twice a week, and each time
the elevator doors
vanished
out of the plush box
a burning author stepped

Finally, it slammed
me shut
inside a worn manuscript
shabby at the edges
from excessive
shipping
into the unsolicited

bins of the world
and back again;
out on the street
I undid the binding
and poems rained
upwards
between the tall
frozen lakes of the
buildings
infecting no one

2. SATAN

A man arose out of the sidewalk—
his skin and his clothes
were the color of pavement.
In his baggy trousers
with his long pointy stick,
he seemed to be walking
among graves, spearing
wrappers and secrets and wills
and what could not be set down in words.

Early Spring

Birds, like black magnolias, burst
at every window into bloom,
ruffling their sleek bodies on boughs
that are still bare. Only far away
is a faint row of maples beginning
to green in an Impressionist landscape
that is probably too sweet, but that
I wish we could frame and hang.
You read hard books all day like poems
and in the middle of a strenuous thought
(does one's arm rising = raising one's arm?)
disappear out the door, whistling
to birds who answer your fond mimicry
with more. Later, when I hear their song
or the next day, after you have gone
and I hear them, my heart trills note
after note, and I rush out
to find you by your piercing call.

Sour Grapes

Dear Sir—only you are a poet
and no gentleman and I, too,
am no gentle reader reading you
to see if you are better than I am
or if, perhaps, in my own estimation
I am not a hair better than you:
still, the poems I like are your best,
marred in the last line most often
by an image that doesn't work
or drag me to joy by the throat or
chasten me like a caress.

Kiss

Like the lost mermaid drinking down
the brew that will cost her her tongue
and split her pearled tail in two,
I tilt my head swimming with wine
from the tangled vines you have grown
in my body and in my mind:
at the touch of your heady breath,
I am riven from skull to thigh.

Metamorphosis

Earth settling in my hair
in brown nests, my veins
green and leafing
under thinner skin, new roots
dragging from my feet, I step
between fashion plates
and buildings, into a shop
full of dresses that go
over my head, pinning
their weird patterns on me,
sheathing my trunk as I stand
wooden before gold mirrors
with a hem at my thigh
and begin to be bought
by beauty I can buy.

Face Cream

Massaging with firm upward strokes napalm
over the cheekbones and up into the area
around the eyes, I watch my face
like a fire along the subway tracks light
the way for the revolution

My husband with his severed penis in his mouth
and his arms and legs chopped off
watches the late show and waits for me
in bed where they left him

Helen

Turned out of an orphanage at fourteen by nuns
to work like a house serf in a pious household
and be beaten as she scrubbed, kept prisoner there
for eight years, while other girls were marrying
or primping—I ask myself what I hate her for.
But the hate is there, no doubt unraveling
something vital inside, while my bone knits.
Her own cracked skin is thin, and her red fingers hurt
too much to have her wash my hair, though she is
my nurse, and there's not much else she can do
with my leg stuck in a cast and the baby not yet born
for her to handle roughly, or confuse
with her bad grammar: "Your husband's pipes
are laying everywhere." She brings with her a gallery
of past employers, dull portraits hung on velvet,
to strut by smartly in her white uniform
and polish off with poison anecdotes.
I picture us at her next job, transformed
into two swine, but wonder why I should feel suddenly
—my pink cheeks stretched around a juicy apple—
so piggish, sitting beside you in that gilt frame.

After the Reading

i

Push in the eyes of the doll
the world is. She is not real,
the whore.
I saw her fifteen years ago
stout and middle-aged;
tonight she was barely twenty
and could not stop touching
her hair.

ii

In Russia, the poets commit
suicide,
at bedtime, disappear
like good children. Here,
cadavers persevere,
never leave
the party.

iii

And the editors
worse than the poets
are poets!
They will not shake your hand
or glance at you
without suspicion,
describing the slim chance.

iv

Falling
from a great height
my tears
upset you.
You waited up
to find out how it went.
I could have slept
mute as my pillow
were there not strewn syllables
like stones
to lay my head on.

Michael Furey

constantly meeting
him
in the glimmering faces of
boys on subways or in
Chock full o' Nuts on the
stool opposite
someone bent eating
defensively
so that I could not eat
the sandwich
in front of me
today
his fat ghost plump
with eating
my years full of his leanness
burst

The Uncertainty of the World

I don't go to fortune tellers
so I'd go, presumably, to a statistics
expert, someone good on probabilities—
a girl has to know what's going on.
And I'd say to this logic-evidence-inference
man, I'd say, I don't like this idea
of the chances are good, because
when the chances are good it turns out to be
a big fat disguise for the fact
that it's no sure thing
and then I lose so how good
could my chances be?

Arsène Lupin

laying your ear to my
navel, you crack me
like a safe.
nothing of mine is safe.
my dreams stashed
in green bundles
topple
into your hands,
heirlooms
wrapped in velvet
slide undone:
                    diamonds
I've kept hidden
since the world changed
smudge
with your breath, even
the sealed envelope
not to be opened until
after my death
is gone: you've taken
everything, and left
inside of me
your fingerprints

Island

Toothless men on a bench on the island
between the gulf streams of traffic
where I was caught between lights—
"Cutcha hair, girlie? Tonite?"
—old codgers and geezers
who could not embrace a living soul,
smoking their fingerstubs in a sea
of car fumes, urinating against the dark
with an inch of garden hose,
sitting in limbo close to
red and green stars and the amber
moon's exhaust, shipwrecked
forever in pulchritude:
they watched me cross in my expensive
clothes, grab an ephemeral
cab and disappear
as savagely as if it were a hearse
they'd never hail, shady
guardians of our being here, soiled
gardeners of glitter and cement.
After I reach my destination, I shall
float back to them, time turning
me over, as waves make love to the dead.

Dusk

The parked cars in double rows going crosstown
are buttons on a dress I plan to wear
and have laid out across my bed
in preparation for your
undoing.

Titania

It hurts as much
to love an
ass
as anyone.

Neptune

                              you stood
behind me in the bathroom mirror
and combed my wet hair out
in long thin lines to my
shoulders
while the moisture on the glass
wept
at your awkward
pains
to dress my hair
as if each streaming strand was
sacred to you   and the steam
incense

but in the morning when a poem
caught me
in its net that needed mending
instantly
and I asked you to compare two lines
you snapped
before untangling me your half-wife
mermaid
struggling in seaweed   seed pearls
escaping
like air   to set me right

Maiden Aunt

Multiplying venom
seventy-odd years, or more,
emaciated with cancer
she could live on now for years
in slowly yellowing
splendor,
wearing her empty hanging dresses
to rare family occasions
where she was silent, coiled, not speaking
spitefully of
you, still separated
from your husband, and of Zsa Zsa Gabor.

Pattern

It was four hours of fog to the labor room
where I faced you with all premeditated
expressions driven away by each great moment
—except one nurse said afterwards that I kept
giving the baby away, to her, and she wanted it!
a young old maid, her raw resentments
hid by her gentle massaging fingers
—and I hit hard with my fists in all directions.

You told me of a Chinese rug you didn't buy
from an antique dealer, which was like a river
streaming under a bridge, the pattern on it,
so that no matter where you stepped, you were
immersed to your waist in Chinese waters, steeped
from the chest up in breathless ether:
hearing of it, and after, a graceful rod
yanks fish out of me like live regrets.

Centuries later, weightless, new-ribbed, wheeling
a Buddha through crowds of idolatrous strangers,
with you beside me and one more whole person
to transact, in time, between us, the long
figured carpet of our years to come unrolling
for blocks and city blocks ahead of us
—too many people treading on it to tell the design—
we watch the smiles bob on and off her cheeks like
                                traffic lights.

Oh, Autumn Is

Oh, Autumn is an old woman who paints
Cheeks onto her cheeks, lips onto her lips,
And on a gray day mopes about the house
Wearing a cobweb shawl that the trees knit.

IRT

dangerously leaning impatient for
the vacuous lovemaking of rough wind-
suck
and the noise
thrown over my head like a blanket
the right train
          comes
we stare by each other
at the glazed panes streaked
indecipherably
          our lives
          sewn like valuables
          into the lining of our skin
          burning holes
          through

Mink Coat

like the satin lining
of some mink
I might have received
as a famous
dancer
with diamonds in the pockets
and long-
stemmed roses to surprise me
in the sleeves
his trembling body
covers me
with applause

Beach

cars litter the shore like empty soda cans
buoying the eye in a blue
sheen of mermaid's
hair

the streets are wrinkles in wet sand
between wet rocks the ocean has
washed over and
left bare

the early morning stragglers stranded here
like bathers in a tub
with all the water
gone

look timidly around them at their sheer
crossing of vitreous china
filled with
dawn

Winter Birds

The small birds hop on spiders through the snow
or swing from suet strung up in the trees
for them to torture with their beaks
into shapes of sinners dangling in hell.
If we move a muscle they fly away
to bud a nearby tree with their tight
wings, waiting, innocent as spring,
to dip sharp beaks into the shrinking fat
or travel on the snow leaving no print.
We stand stone-still at the edge of the room
watching for the male woodpecker's red
mating spot to show, and I want to shout,
"Let us not give up meat, but tear at it, and eat,
and give our own flesh up to the sharp teeth of love."

Sickbed

wanting to do it
effortlessly
like angels shimmying
in shimmering heat
without these obdurate
bodies in the way

your fever fretting my skin
scaring me to feel hot
hands on my bones
as if death might yet come for me

sebaceous fires burning in my thighs
clenched   climbing
to your hard groin where our
torn cries hang
enduring as heads on pikes
picketing time

The City

i

Sitting on his lap, on his buses
and subways, in taxis,
I am sinful, and alive.

ii

His voice roars, or is so gentle,
skyscrapers full of women
weep.

iii

All the shops on Broadway
miss him when winter
stops his walks.
I stand in front of the vulgar
windows full of underwear
with holes
for nipples and behinds to show,
naked in my revealing
new red lace
longing for him.

Her Sleep

Wasps or hornets rattle on the sills
and fill the vestibule with danger;
my daughter, rocked by lullabies
of wind, naps inside mosquito netting
like a bride before the veil is lifted
for the rough world to injure with its kiss.
Still a wound my husband cannot enter
since the child departed from me—her dream
drags its belly, suns on a honeyed spoon—
seeing her sleep, I am stung.

Together

I saw him glance at me before the light
caught in his glasses and I could not see.

I noticed his belly especially, its vast
confidence—as if all of the women he had at once
were in it—his bald
intelligence.

At the end of the evening I touched
his jacket's sleeve to ask a question.
When he looked round at me
severely,
my shoes' amber buckles clashed with my red dress.

Rendezvous

Summoned from a dream of your summoning
by your cry, I steal out of bed and leave
my doting husband deaf to the world.
We meet, couple, and cling, in the dim light—
your soft mouth tugs and fills and empties me.
We stay that way a long time it seems, till
on your brimming face, where milky drops glide,
I see my body's pleasure flood and yawn.
We turn each other loose to sleep. Smiling
your smile of innocence, I return
to the bed of your begetting, and a man's warm side.

The Local

a drowned hulk
in slacks and exploding
high heels
often adrift after dark absently towing
some small dried-out husk
of a man
up sidestreets against the wind
wordlessly
tied to her by his own delicate
spittle
at rush hour she leans against the tiled wall
on the bottom stair
waiting for whoever steps through her sliding
doors tapping with his cane car after
car lurching through her

Solomon

your anger strikes at me
with metallic arms
whirring the night air
in our bedroom
like propellers
you must go
bearing the child I bore
without me
to your mother
I touch your tense back
as you stare
programmed to fulfill
her wishes
I must give away my half
or she will cut you in two
but I am not your real
mother

Jungle

in the savage hubbub of bare
breasts
under sweaters, each pair
jingling a different
tune
from the others, I watch
your eyes
leap
at the powerful leopard
in leotards at the yellow butterfly
with trembling wings
silent inside my bra
my sucked breasts
bask
in retirement
and all our plump children hang
from them
firm
as the hotel sphinx
with great granite breasts miles
apart
crouched with her twin
cudgels at the door—

I remember
one morning running from side to
side of our bed hiding
your erection

under a giant quilt while half-
asleep you gave car-keys
or directions to our
friend
a mad monkey in the jungle
shielding her mate
with leaves
naked in bed I cling
to a drowned ship while you love me
with your whole body like a
shark
and my rollicking bones
litter
the horsehair mattress, the sidewalks
the sea
where lost breasts float
and bob that have been torn off
by some jealous instrument
by me

Call

Desire in me to be an unattractive
old scratchy-voiced lady, or a man
wanting a girl from a lit phone booth,
or some relative of yours whose voice
you hate, who always greets you at this hour,
is speechless, while your voice hangs up.

News

watching the
broadcast
from Cambodia
there is blood
shed in my lap
like a first
menses

Divorce

salmon
struggling back
to the mouth
of their native
stream
the female
intoxicated
shoveling with her tail
on the stony bottom
to clear a nest
for her young
the male ejaculates
a distinct visible
shadow of his pleasure
as she swims under him
to egg him on
after three days
of supreme excitement
they suffer a
transformation
and die
unless they cannot leap
the falls
and lie torn
on the rocks
unable to mate
downstream

unable to mate
after thirty-three years
of trying to
jump
to break the
surface
of each other's
resistance
impossible to scale
or swim
against the current
beached
living apart

Witness

I long to see myself as an old old
woman
as for the cruel murders I will see
under my own eyes
I will smile over it, no
I will fling myself into the alley
before dawn
where the butcher's stunned trashcans
in too tight girdles stand
fat with bones
and wrap my arms around my knees
or dance
and induce him with my long legs in gray
opaque panty hose
to let me ride beside him near the
mirror

Samson

from the door she heads for my legs
and stands between them
blind

her curls with no power but the power
to curl
she mows me down

March Snow

The wet snow sticks to the branches, clinging
Like a naked girl with arms and legs wrapped
Around a boy who will not marry her.
Soon he will straighten like a birch and leave
Her to her tears, or shake her off when Spring
At last returns and with green eyes seeks him.
At dusk, when you come home, the fierce blackbirds
That churn your hair with silver feet, will fall
Into my lap: while I make much of them,
The mourning dove I've fed will fly away.

The Money Room

When girls come, you can take them into it
and leave some of your wife's old furs around
with cash pushing through the frayed silk linings
and the stuffed pockets spilling onto the floor
that rises like a mermaid, drowning them
luxuriously in the toils of her chrome hair.
You can go in there yourself after a shower
and roll around on the turf till you're all dry,
and breathe in the pine ink like mountain air:
this is not all that you have, it's what's left over.
You can live in the world of impoverished people, then.
Or die, and be rich forever, immortally
embalmed in the neuroses of expensive Jewish girls,
wrapped in their dark complaints like wavy hair,
receiving the perpetual interest of their tears.

War

1

undeclared
comes home to
me, limping, its face
reconstructed by surgeons

2

the boys all from deep
in the abdomen
have died
killing the easy produce
of women squatting
over rags spread in the field:
dim aubergines wiped out

3

like the greenbacks
on the stoops of weekend
sidestreets
where the men in threes
empty their pockets
and loose cash
thick as leaves
lies motionless for a moment
changing hands,
the dead
are spent on whores

Hiroshima Night

we sat listening, strung by dune grasses and horse
flies, appraising the barefoot faces of strangers;
sand winced in the grains of your expression, the red sun
flayed the steel rims of your civilized glasses, the moon
lighted the way for the gulls to bomb the ocean:
survivors, dead set on jail, hardened as convicts
to the selfish stars, but when you brushed
a fly off my leg with a freckled hand, our lavish fire-
bombs clustered again like grapes in my blue veins:
people boiling in the asphalt of their own streets drowned.

Griselda

Her nights of crying finally doused
the lights in the upper stories
of the buildings, beheaded
to a queer silence
in which, sitting still, staring into the dark,
I could hear her weeping.
                              My own eyes filled
with blood I wanted to shed,
my voice crusted to a razor edge, sharpened
continuously by her compassion.

She was the only one who could read his handwriting
as we went through cartons of incriminating
poems for the lawyers,
her mute pain deciphering
obscenities he shared with other women;
or what he thought of his three children:
cutting badly, like a blunt
Haiku.

Anger
locked out of her bedroom
threw wild parties
in me.

Like a huddle of surly
dykes turning-on,
I sucked in
hate
that couldn't penetrate
her lips.

Her refugee English never took
its apron off
in this different country;
the old world clung
in kerchiefs, softness, willingness
to scrub, and somewhere
behind the blue eyes—huge, clear—
scenes from her German childhood:
they hung her
from a halter in icy water
to teach her how to swim, her father
killed himself.

In her feminine room filled with photos
and prints of Madonnas, and a Brueghel
that a lover liked, sentimental attachment
like a halo around everything,
and music going,

the three of us settle among deep quilts
—my friend, my husband, and me—
to talk,
and love has got his hands on us
though we can't see his face
or remember his voice.

Long after, inscribed
in an old book
of tales
of unknown origins,
I found her
name.

Lady Cardinal

A coy mistress with coral beak, puffed up
with her own beauty, dragging a gorgeous
scarlet train: scandal and drabs attend her,
sparrow about her as she condescends
to peck at seed. Buried under the snow,
old morsels to glut on: the proud thing flew
from irate parents to a bed of down
and rose, rumpled, stuck with feathers, her plump
body winged, her blush become her lover.

Mary

I will look in the mirrors on candy
machines and on certain walls
on Broadway for someone
motherly, invisible,
and I will give her my breasts
and instructions and say
these are not for husbands or lovers
and as long as the child has this
in his mouth you almost
disappear
and I will go off with long hair
like a boy
swinging my hips under the afternoon
marquees bearing my name
in feature after feature
and I will walk on the backs of taxis
and limousines stalled in traffic
until I am raped by the horses of the mounted
police and brought to the stable
for a second
birth.

Your Looks

even a waitress said once
you looked like Gregory Peck
not that it mattered what
you looked like
I made a terrible mistake
admitting
I'd even love you
fat
when I looked at you
all legs and nose at some
uncomfortable desk
or leaning back in a
swivel chair
I could see you had no idea
why
it did what it did to me

In Wonderland

suddenly after one cookie too many
alice has shot up
out of earshot almost of the mad
party
that is for some infant's birthday now
that she
has grown up

even going to a shrink
there is no
going back
while forward lies a deep hole
full of no
falling

A Man Who Sucks His Thumb

a man who sucks his thumb
with long matted hair
in disheveled ringlets
and a hard shy body
like a statue he always thought
too fat

easing the paint on, not scrubbing
lapping it on
on the giant canvases on the floor
between the thin strips
of masking tape, intuitive
as color

or views, sidereal, splattered,
the local talent from a cab girls
he lets slip through his twisted
fingers that a friend rolled an urn on
once years before his missing teeth were
knocked out

Day of Reckoning

i

Husband, I have
your love, your name,
your child.
What is left
for me to strive for?

ii

Today
every poem I read
is good,
stretched out
on the prayer rug
while mine
are being judged.

iii

*Gotten at last, with labour
and long toil*:
I am writing
my acceptance speech.

iv

Looking back disappointed
on yesterday's hope
must we hate
our euphoria?

v

In suspense
strong as maidenhead
I wait
perfumed and ready,
but no bridegroom comes.

vi

Even coming this close
to being chosen!
He has till now only
touched you,
whose very existence
in some other room
makes you quake.

vii

We go to sleep together
in the dark
like strangers in an inn
after a hard journey
too weary to speak
but our bones talk.

Emperor of Lies

The fat Emperor of Lies who wore bow ties
and threadbare sports jackets
wrote a book on Aesthetics.

His lady-friends loved sadists. I spoke
to one or two of them myself, bare-breasted
at the time, he told me after.

And so, though there were those who questioned
whether he liked boys, or how any woman
could like him, it seemed feasible:

I liked him. The marvelous thing was how
he masturbated with knives, thrusting
them double-edged into each trusting back.

Palinode

hurt turns into
blood
in a warm hurry
as if your whole body
blurred
and the hurt burned
in the false image
overlapping
all the skin
tingles a little bit
electrocuted
the false self
criminal
worshiper of idols
tastes its poison
like a last
meal

Cinderella

The master stroke was the mustache.
I had
sideburns, and wore
one of the expensive ties
your mother buys.
In the full-length mirror, I loved
myself.
I was myself, I could put on a man's
coat—hair chopped off
by my father's hat—and stride
to the party. No need to pose
or please
or try to steal a dozen husbands
from their wives.
I put the lipstick on you
though your lips went slack
or, taut, curled in too much
and disappeared.
I brushed on rouge, blush
pink, lilac
eye shadow, and powdered your nose.
You seemed old, a big woman

with whom too many men
had been
emasculated.
We pulled on Bernadette's ripped
panty hose
and stuck men's socks in her bra
under an itchy dress.
You were miserable, you squirmed.
You carried my displaced headache
in your purse.

Jennifer Suite

1. ORIGINAL SIN

Her big eyes
plumped
into her siren's face
will slide
out of their shapely boats
and, on the carpet, spill
black ink.

2. SHOE

To hear some masculine voice
disfigure itself with
love,
she holds my black shoe up
to her ear
and with her dark plum eyes
mulls over
the sweet noise.

3. TRAUMA

This morning when I crawled
back into bed with you while
the baby walked around it
holding on, laughing her head
off over the high peaks of
quilt at her hidden
parents, we did it.

4. INFLATION

Her eyes like black 89c cherries
—one pumpernickel beautymark
on her McIntosh cheek—
she looks at the fruitman
from her seat on the basket
as if to say, I have never
seen such prices!

Newsletter

meeting the ladies my tail between my legs
I sit on the nursery chair while Neptune's son kicks
and his daughter rides a sea horse her chin jutting
in self-consciousness among the morning 4's

whose mothers explain who they are and how many
are theirs and where the others are and ask
"do you write poems at home . . . ?"
pulling my hair with their tortoise comb

Room 669

a man I know
is in the hospital
with a blood clot
traveling
under the bandages
of the leg they
operated on
he thinks he will stay
a long time
and then be moved up
to geriatrics
near his bed
there is a memorandum
Mademoiselle would like to
interview him on where
famous people go
for vacations

Shopper's Paradise

Like a supermarket, you never ran out.
Your shelves were full of goods
—pickles, rolls, smoked oysters, Tragedy plums—
to go straight into my basket
and home to open and eat.
Now, without warning, you say,
"It's a holiday. I'm closed."
I am swept out long aisles of hungry women.

Curtains

heavily made-up his man's face
that had been blue a day ago
when you called him and called
him from the next bed
to find out how he was
smiled
        like a showgirl
slowly arising from a pink satin
cake that was taking its last bite
of him

Wedding Day

I open the lid to the sing-
song
of sirens and one jade
bus
like a brooch
pulls up to the round
corner
of my breast, I pin it
on
and then another comes, jeweled
with ads
dressing me in joyful prints to meet him,
the bridegroom
is laid out on the subway platform
like a star
in outer space, like a dead
soldier
his white face the moon
after acne,
on the track at his feet
they are dragging away a tin can
and departing, I must take off
my coat
to marry him, so he may rise
a stranger

Wait!

I've found your tie for you
in the disordered closet and the baby is hopping
with egg on her face to kiss you at the door
and our powdered lovely girl who speaks
French is perfuming the house with strong odors
and cologne and I am in the middle of
seeing you for the first time and there is no time
to get married for we are six years
gone

Horns

that could flower into green
antlers
impacted in his velvet brow,
that part I love in thrilling suede
dangles over me like a god

that part I love in thrilling suede
dangles over me like a god,
horns that could flower into green
antlers
impacted in his velvet brow

Manhattan

You are my driver, in your
hands my wheel with its bumps
slides, my radio plays
loud, drumming holes
in the soft heads of girls,
when you touch me, when you
blow smoke rings inside
my face crowded with rain
on the way to work,
when you think about some-
thing else, the light
on my ceiling is out, I wear
your plates, love, mister,
new york, they found your
credit card in the crack
between my thighs, they never got
your fishing rods out of me
from behind,
I am sitting this minute
in a dangerous lot.

Salomé

                              you sit
under two coats while I dance before you
distorting robe after robe for the hospital
proud of the great swelling that makes you wince
in the negligee department of Lord & Taylor's;
at home, my feet bound in my own hair, encumbered
by a mile-wide blue-veined cummerbund, I think
you will swallow the baby if labor begins
now with your mouth open between my legs
and I will pass out cigars and smoke your pipe
and buy you a velvet kimono to be wondered at
in

Luck

Lesbian,
I want her
to come now
and console me
for all the others,
men,
and women too,
who have enjoyed her
before me,
all younger and smiling
on book jackets
as if some pimply
muse
had put them there,
instead of this
sweet
double-jointed
whore
who can screw (in two
senses)
but not read.

Riverside Park

the park
seen from above on bicycles
flashes like a basin
filled with cold sun I've never tasted
impinging
like a loud knock at the unlocked door
of a bedroom
where we were under covers
dressed, perfumed, in each other
like spring and autumn fallen in love
this beauty is an interruption
to that good darkness
where my closed eyes catch your eyes
closed
where the tangle of our legs
passing long boats laden with silver
garbage from the rich lives
in a big city
like this
feels the sperm race dancing to fresh graves

A Fiery Furnace

"O Lord (saide Musidorus) how sharp-witted you are
to hurt your selfe? No (answered he) but it is
the hurt you speake of, which makes me so sharp-witted."

SIR PHILIP SIDNEY, *Arcadia*

1. Meeting

II

Joy lunged from a black jaw.
The ridged roof of its mouth was black.
Our words stood out like vertebrae
On the back of a slender god.

2. Love Letter

In the next room pounding out a love letter
You were hunched the way I love you
Over the harsh machine.

You typed so fast it seemed all underscore.
It was like hemorrhaging
My blood into endearments my blindness sealed.

3. The Only Hand

The only hand I ever held while sleeping
moves in the darkness over my face. My eyelids
tremble, and it comes to my smiling cheeks.

Sometimes with my face somewhere along your ribs
I wonder, do you feel when my smile begins?
You take my hand and fall asleep again.

4. Waking

Exquisitely trampled in a goat-footed dance
my eyes shift left to right to left, openly
watching your narrow eyes watching me.
Unless our dreams get mixed and girls
of yours come meandering into mine
flaunting their alien flesh, like mine,
I like the silence after napping best.

5. A Fiery Furnace

You stand apart in a fiery furnace
Where knowledge of my burning can't ease yours.
You wait, fine brawn poised, all silence
In the dark flame of a stranger's heart.

6. Every Third Thought

We kept our young souls hidden years ago—
above all from each other.
Now every third thought I give you up.
There is too little time to be old ever.

7. Out of Wedlock

In the fierce bomblight strange bodies kiss.
I sit next to snow on our green bench.
Some bastard dream born out of wedlock
Tags along through the snowing day
And sows seeds of violence right and left.

8. Another Light

Momentary blindness seeing you
In another light, feeling suddenly
As if I'd vomited, before the nausea
Swells again, swallowing me up,
Is all the grace I'm granted when I beg.

9. Your Heartbeats

Vulnerable and shrewd almost escaping between ribs
Your heartbeats stammered messages for me
To misconstrue and misconstrue again.
The task of reinterpreting
Skips no beat still.

10. Night

As if a helicopter had lowered me
onto a frozen lake of a land
and throttling off left me
to talk to myself and watch my words
hang like smoke in the air,
I go to bed saying your name.

11. Absence

Without you the days
lengthen like a dead girl's hair
like fingernails of the dead growing
sharp like barbed wire
wrapped around my head: my own thoughts
draw blood.

12. Desire

To be like the snowy pattern
Of town on the steep slope opposite,
Pink morning and evening like the snow,
Not to be lovesick over you squandering
Armfuls of lifetime melting through and through,
Is a desire only yours could prove untrue.

13. Fairy Tale

Long ago in a book I blurred with tears
A little mermaid had such bad luck in love
She turned to foam. For all love's bitterness
When the huge boat smashes against sky
I'd have my mermaid's tail again
And plunge back through pages of rough sea
To where the young prince foundered in the waves
And save him from the fatal girl he wants
And kiss him till he woke up wanting me.

14. An Open Book

In the open book of my life
I can be seen at all hours
Erasing your name;
Only the tissue of those days we spent
Dodging the planets jealous at each touch
Is rubbed so thin now, veins show
My thought.

15. The Crime

Out of love with you for letting me go,
Even at this distance recoiling
As if you stood with the thing around your neck
We could have had, looking so hateful now
Stone dead, the aborted form of our two lives,
I turn to run, and sink knee-deep in corpses:
        The days I murdered mourning for your sake
With one withering voice cry *Hypocrite!*

16. Epithalamion

This weekend the epithalamion
You may be listening to yourself compose,
Watching the tense girl at rest under your skin
Or at your side—myself, my own ghost
Startling mirrors with my sudden shape
Or pair of eyes—from room to room, haunts me.

1. The Tower

Afraid because a woman alone
Is not a woman, and because
Your touch left me too real
(Before you left, my shining knight,
And locked me in this tower)
To make-believe making love:
I let down my long hair to no one
Through the bars.

2. Drinking Song

Her face like a goblet full of wine
Was raised to him as to a light
Newly crimson with laughter
The years would drink slowly
Or at one gulp;
                    drink that,
Before the rare rose turns
And vinegar burns your lower lip, you
Girl in the mirror, attend to your glass.

3. Your Visit

for Wendy

One Egyptian eye opens in our bed
Voluptuous with sleep—O warm dark moon
Of morning. Good morning sweet sister
We say, entangled in our Persian bedding.

As in your dream's fearful choreography
My lonely trembling vibrates into strength,
I brave chill sun motes mottling one leg
And, barefoot, love life and your open face.

4. Elijah

An angel touches his lips to the wine.
We pulled up a chair for the absent stranger.
Absolutely expecting a miracle to happen
I watched his glass through the good smells of dinner,
Until in the middle of the heavy eating
The angel took a sip, and then was gone:
As you, my friend, have touched your lips to mine.

5. Sentimental Visit

Lying face down on the grass, my thoughts
grope like two hands in apron pockets
to where my young grandmother went
to forget her life in peace and quiet.

With thick lips a gush of rain kisses
sentimental words that speak like scars
on the stone forehead of someone dead.
No good-bye can be said. I run for it.

6. Blackout

You held my hand in front of the side-entrance.
There was almost as much darkness as when
Heaven opened that year on my birthday
And filled my lap with trading cards.
No one my age was outside with her father.
You hadn't said, but I knew if a bomb fell
The pocket you would catch it in.

7. My Grandmother

The subject came up about talent—I was wolfing down
The generous portions served in your house—
And you said, "If I could only write them
The way they happened, I have stories to tell . . ."
—Your hands like silk that took away my headaches,
You, the best cook in the world and more
Beautiful than anyone you played poker with—
But none of your stories ended; not one so much as
Hinted that my grandmother could die
In the middle of her own life, scarcely knowing mine.

8. Every Man

In love with every man whose eyes
My eyes won't meet—except in secret
Sometimes (never the way I looked at you
With naked eyes that drew you in
In open love)—though their good looks ignite
This darkness, not one can cross
The fiery moat to take me to his bed.

9. Bus Terminal

"I have my dying to do; you have yours,"
You say, kissing me good-bye. Wearing your amber
Necklace like a lifetime of summers honeying
Around my neck—the Yahrzeit candles burn all night
Hysterical as dreams—worried because
You never sleep, saying with you what good times
We had together for a week!—I kiss you back,
And my father, before the empty bus to the airport
Carries me in numbness through the sequined dark.

10. April Storm

Large empty garbage cans left huddled at the curb
After the garbage truck has come and gone,
Roll wild and rattle in the rising wind.
Rivers of wind fill up with rain.
Tugging at their roots the trees scrape back
And forth against the sky. It stops.
In shafts of light from platinum clouds, God crawls.

11. Sunset

Lying near me on the pillow, my dark hair
Like the shrub of winding thickets on the hill
—The ripe sun a berry caught in it—
Breathes back perfume put on once for you.

1. Granite Dawn

Cracking the granite dawn below
squat men wielding a yellow machine
jitter a row of houses with its purr;
each night the first kiss of yours
I dream, from my own dream, jolts me.

2. Recovery

A hairpin slides like an insect down my back.
Diving down between cushions
Recovering it,
Something else evades my fingertips.
My hand pulls back:
When I lost you and got lost, it may be
What I found.

3. Proposition

Phrases that have dirt under their nails
Breaking the skin out loud to wonder
Syllables of soot   who I am
Enter the bloodstream:
Venom of no veiled like a nun
Shaking his hand.

4. Solitude

Black wind hurtling against black panes
Folding in sleep far away from me
Carrying my cry through paper walls
Your body a jackknife closing my eyes
—the whole house inches closer to the gorge.

5. Spring

Smudge-pots stand guard in the broken street.
A bee in the dark fur of its flight
noses along the ceiling, dives.
Bearing branches of lilac buds shaking
their tiny fists in my face, I blossom
beautiful and mended like a vase.

6. Tulip

Asleep in the furtive chamber of a flower
swaying above the ground not looking down
I curl up against a bluff of curling petals
my body crushed into impossible repose

7. Discovering Roots

Under the sink one shriveled potato left
to hibernate all winter stuck out blunt
bony fingers that filled the cabinet.
Shrinking from the pale roots groping

in daylight, a skeleton uncoiling
up from damp umber underneath the basin,
something sank in the closet of my flesh.
It had pushed through a plastic bag to do it.

8. To a Horse

Now when we leave the windrows of hay
behind us and canter over the clouds
below and chanting my words mount and whinny
like magic, I'm happy, I'm happy,
sweet mare: I never forget your name.

9. The Stable

On the threshold of the stable smelling
nothing but the square bales of hay and giant
oaks that swallow the white hawk evenings,
I duck under a curtain of flies and approach
the horses like hours standing hours in a row.

10. Evening Ride

Swift cries answering back
the soft threats of dusk
perch overhead on boughs where I can't see;
my own music
creaks from the loving saddle
under me.

11. Pool at the Bottom of a Falls

My hairpins fall out and sink
in the loose green hair
of the watery place
water has wrested from rock
to woo men there.
She splashes me with her tears.

12. Caress

My heart's fill of fireflies kept in a jar
spills summers ago when you touch my breast
punctures to let in air my eyes won't close
catching my breath in your fist

13. Becalmed

Stars trying to keep still all night
fidget in heaven; with one foot dragging
the deep lukewarm, near you

in the smooth lap of dark, lapping
and the lake full of extinguished wishes,
moments of pain surface, face-down, shriveled.

14. Idle Hands

Hurt from hard words you are slow to say
—your hand in mine, is mine—
suffers our idle hands to grasp:
the blind touching the blind, we touch.

15. Aubade

After the night spent of invisible stars,
wide in the horizontal distances
diffused, like my restless hair blown
by the burly wind and scattered
over the bare shoulders of hills, the sun
welcomes you in my arms.

16. Parting

My fingers part the brown sea of your hair.
We stroll on secret feet of laughter safely through:
When the mysterious wave beckons and you go
Sleep deep inside me fledges strong black wings.

17. Nakedness

Your love like velvet, lining
the loose garment of time
I wear next to my skin,

tore at the seams and frayed
threadbare in one season
letting cold in.

18. The Happy End

Studying the sad chronology of poets' lives
(all their years shoved into the staid embraces
of parentheses), up in arms at the happy end
of a youth or age of love—important dates
slip out of mind like liberated men—I finger
fresh misgivings pressed between the pages.